A FIRST AMERICANS BOOK

THE HAUDENOSAUNEE

Virginia Driving Hawk Sneve · Illustrated by Ronald Himler

HOLIDAY HOUSE NEW YORK

A NOTE FROM THE PUBLISHER

This book was originally published under the title of *The Iroquois* in 1995. To update and prepare the book for republication today, we have worked with Hayden Haynes, the director of Onöhsagwë:de' Cultural Center and a member of the Seneca Nation. We hope this book serves as an introduction to some of the first American Nations and that you will continue to explore Haudenosaunee history and culture by visiting the websites listed in the back of the book.

Printed and bound in October 2025 at Toppan Leefung, DongGuan, China.
www.holidayhouse.com
Second Edition
ISBN: 978-0-8234-5860-8 | 1 3 5 7 9 10 8 6 4 2 (hardcover)
ISBN: 978-0-8234-6200-1 | 1 3 5 7 9 10 8 6 4 2 (paperback)

Library of Congress has cataloged the prior edition as follows:
Sneve, Virginia Driving Hawk.
The Iroquois / by Virginia Driving Hawk Sneve ; illustrated by
Ronald Himler. – 1st ed.
p. cm. – (A First Americans book)
Includes bibliographical references and index.
ISBN 0-8234-1163-X
1. Iroquois Indians – Juvenile literature. [1. Iroquois Indians.
2. Indians of North America.] I. Himler, Ronald, ill. II. Title.
III. Series: Sneve, Virginia Driving Hawk. First Americans book.
E99.I7S625 1995 94-3748 CIP AC
973'.04975 — dc20

EU Authorized Representative: HackettFlynn Ltd, 36 Cloch Choirneal,
Balrothery, Co. Dublin, K32 C942, Ireland. EU@walkerpublishinggroup.com

The Haudenosaunee Confederacy in Colonial New York, Pre-1640
CANADA
NEW YORK
Lake Ontario
Lake Erie
MOHAWK
ONEIDA
ONONDAGA
CAYUGA
SENECA
Hudson River
PENNSYLVANIA

Creation

Today, the Haudenosaunee is made up of several different peoples. There are many versions of how the Haudenosaunee came to be, depending on who is telling the story. This is just one of the stories.

Once, long ago in the Sky World, a woman was gathering seeds and berries when a giant tree was uprooted, leaving a hole. Sky Woman fell through the hole and plunged down toward where there was no land. There was only water, in which the fish and the animals swam. As Sky Woman fell, swans and geese flying over the water caught her with their wings.

"What shall we do with Sky Woman?" the birds asked. "She cannot fly like us, and she cannot swim. She needs a place to stand."

The creatures held a council and decided that they should dive into the sea and bring up some soil from the bottom. When they did, all failed except for muskrat. He was able to bring up a tiny bit of mud.

"But where shall we put it?" the animals wondered.

"On my back," turtle answered.

So the animals placed the bit of mud on turtle's back. It grew and grew until it became the earth. There, Sky Woman was set down. She dropped the seeds she had carried from the Sky World, and they grew into all of the plants and trees of the earth.

In this legend, the Sky Woman's children later became the Haudenosaunee.

The Haudenosaunee Confederacy

The Haudenosaunee peoples are the Mohawk, Oneida, Onondaga, Cayuga, and Seneca Nations. They once occupied what is now the state of New York. Haudenosaunee means "those who build the longhouse" or "people of the longhouse," because they lived in long, rectangular houses. Their enemy, the Algonquins, may have given them the name Iroquois, meaning "bad or terrifying man." Or it may have come from another enemy tribe's word meaning "snake" or "real snake." The French adopted the name "Iroquois."

Long before the French and other white men came in the early 1600s, the Haudenosaunee fought among themselves. Many oral traditions say that over a thousand years ago, a man called Peacemaker had a vision of

all people living happily together. This man may have been of the Huron tribe, or a Mohawk, but he met Ayonwatha, or Hiawatha, an Onondaga who also wanted peace. The two men persuaded the Nations to work together and take up the path of peace. They asked them to form a confederacy, or league, so that they could meet together to discuss issues that concerned all of them. Peacemaker uprooted a great white pine, and the warriors threw their weapons into the hole. The tree was replanted, and fifty chiefs linked hands around the trunk to hold it up if it fell. This act stood for the idea that all the Nations together were stronger than when apart.

The Haudenosaunee ceased fighting among themselves and helped each other in battles with enemy tribes.

A meeting of fifty chiefs

The league was organized in the same way a longhouse was. Several families lived in a single longhouse, each in their own section with their own or sometimes a shared firepit and hearth.

In a similar fashion, all five Nations belonged to the league, but each had its separate place. The Mohawk became the "keepers of the Eastern Door," the Seneca the "keepers of the Western Door," the Onondaga, in the center of the territory, were "keepers of the Council Fire." In about 1722, the Tuscarora Nation of North Carolina joined the league due to forced removal by white settlers. The league then became the Six Nations.

The Haudenosaunee confederate council came to be known as the Grand Council. It was made of fifty chiefs. The council was divided into two bodies: the elder brothers, the Mohawk, Seneca, and Onondaga; and the younger brothers, the Cayuga and Oneida. The names of the founders of the league are still used today. The leadership titles have been passed down through the Haudenosaunee women.

In the early 1600s, the Haudenosaunee acquired guns from the Dutch. With the weapons, the league kept peace in their homelands. The league also controlled boat travel on the Great Lakes and the fur trade in Haudenosaunee territory.

The notched staff was used by a Haudenosaunee sachem to list the members of the Grand Council.

Men

Besides being powerful warriors, the Haudenosaunee men were skilled hunters. On foot, they silently stalked deer or drove moose and caribou into the water, where hunters in canoes killed them.

To lure game, the hunters made calls that sounded exactly like those of animals. Sometimes they disguised themselves with skins and lay in wait for their prey along trails or by water holes. Several men organized hunting parties to drive deer into fenced barriers, where they killed the animals with bows and arrows. The hunters only killed what they needed to survive.

The Haudenosaunee liked to fish too. They used spears, bows and arrows, or lures and hooks to catch fish.

Haudenosaunee men made all their own tools and weapons. They fashioned arrowheads from flint, jasper, or slate. They used springy wood, such as shagbark hickory, white ash, cedar, or white oak, to make bows. They set round stones into wooden handles to make war clubs.

The trees in the forests also supplied wood for carving dishes. The men and women carved wooden bowls, ladles, and spoons. In addition, they built lightweight, swift canoes by fastening elm bark to wooden frames. They made the canoes waterproof by sealing the seams with a mixture of spruce gum and charcoal. And they used the wood of the forest and rawhide strips to make snowshoes for traveling in deep snow.

The Haudenosaunee men wore deerskin shirts, leggings, breechcloths, and moccasins. Some of the men shaved their heads completely, leaving only a small amount of hair on top.

Haudenosaunee spoons

Lacrosse racket and ball

When Haudenosaunee men weren't hunting, fishing, or working on crafts, they relaxed by playing games. One of their favorites is known today as lacrosse, a name from the French. The Haudenosaunee were the first players and have several names for the game, including the Creator's Game and the Medicine Game. The Onondaga call it Dehoñtjihgwa'és and the Mohawk call it Tewa'á:raton.

Each player had a racket with which he caught and threw a ball. Trained teams attempted to throw the ball into goals set at the end of large fields. The first team to score three goals won. Teams from different Nations would compete. The people who watched often placed bets on which team would win. The players carefully discussed plans for winning the game, which was fun as well as useful training for war.

Food

Husking pins

Kernel scraper

Mealing stone used for grinding corn

The eastern woodland not only had plenty of game and fish, but it had fertile soil as well. Corn is so important to the Haudenosaunee that they call it different names by different Nations. They hold a festival when the seeds are planted, another when the young corn is green, and finally one for the harvest of ripe ears. They plant squash and beans along with the corn. These vegetables are called the "three sisters," and their spirits protect the crops. Besides giving corn a special name, some Haudenosaunee call squash "supporter of life."

Food was roasted over fires in sunken pits or boiled in clay pots. Corn was eaten on the cob or in soup. The Haudenosaunee grind corn and bake it into cakes to this day.

Making maple sugar

Sometimes they mixed cornmeal with maple sugar, dried berries, or chopped dried meat. They often boiled corn with wood ashes. This made it more nutritious and easier to remove the loosened hulls. The remaining corn became hominy. It was washed and boiled until tender. Hominy, corn, and beans were mixed together into succotash, a hearty dish that white settlers added to their diet.

Nuts and berries and other wild plants were also part of Haudenosaunee meals. The wild strawberry, the earliest fruit of the year, was a special favorite. In the spring, the Haudenosaunee held a festival to celebrate the feast of ripe berries.

Spring was sugaring time. The Haudenosaunee had a dance to bring warm weather so that the maple sap would flow. At the end of the sugaring, the Haudenosaunee held a ceremony to give thanks.

Women

Clan symbols from a variety of Nations

Women played an important part in Haudenosaunee society. Haudenosaunee heritage and inheritance were traced through them. Even though the members of the league council were men, the leadership was passed through the female line. If any member of the council wasn't fulfilling his duties, the women had the power to remove him from office.

Every family belonged to a clan. Each clan, named after an animal or bird, depending on the Nation, had a headwoman. Before the headwoman died or gave up her position, she carefully chose the woman who would take her place. Her choice had to be approved by the clan's women, then the clan chiefs, and finally the league council.

Although Haudenosaunee men were responsible for clearing the fields, women mainly planted the crops. The women sowed the seeds and tended the growing plants. They were in charge of the harvest that would keep the Haudenosaunee from starving during the winter.

The women prepared all the food for daily meals. They also dried or smoked it so that it would not spoil during the cold months. The food was stored in containers made from birch bark or underground in pits.

Haudenosaunee mothers tanned hides, then used them to sew and decorate clothing and moccasins for their families. They sewed leather by punching holes in it with a bone awl, a pointed tool. Then they laced layers together with thread made from plant fibers. Their skirts and sleeveless dresses were fashioned from soft, tanned deerskins. Tougher tanned leather was made into leggings and soft-soled moccasins. The women decorated the clothing with porcupine quills.

Burden frame

It was mounted on the woman's back and tied around her head with long straps. The extra rope at the top was used to tie in whatever was being carried.

Container made from corn husks

Women made baskets for gathering roots and plants. They carried the baskets on their backs, fastened to a leather band or woven strap of plant fibers around their foreheads. This tumpline was used to steady the pack and free the women's hands to carry other things. Mothers and grandmothers used cedar bark, rushes, corn husks, and cattails to weave mats and storage bags for the longhouse. Some women made coiled clay pots for cooking and storage.

Haudenosaunee women had many tasks, but they also found time for games. Teams of women played a ball game in which a curved stick was used to toss and catch a buckskin ball filled with sand. The women also enjoyed a game called shinny. It was a little like hockey.

Children

Haudenosaunee babies, from birth until they began to walk, spent much of their time in cradleboards. A cradleboard was made of a flat board with a footboard at the bottom and a bowed strip of wood at the top. This protected the baby's face. A leather covering held the baby in place. The mother tied the cradleboard to a strap around her forehead or shoulders when she carried her baby. She used the strap to hang the cradleboard on a limb or peg in the house. That way the baby was safe while the mother worked.

Girls cared for their younger brothers and sisters. If a girl had no little ones in her family, she took care of her baby cousins, whom she called brother or sister. Older girls went with the women to plant the seeds, weed the fields, and harvest the crops. Girls learned to cook by watching the women in the longhouse and by helping their mothers. When the women made clothes, they gave the girls small pieces of leather to sew into garments for their corn-husk dolls.

From an early age, Haudenosaunee boys played with little bows and arrows. At first, a boy learned to hunt by playing at stalking birds and small game and by practicing with his miniature weapons. By age eight or nine, he was able to bring rabbits and birds home to his mother. Older boys formed hunting parties with others their age. Often, they took younger brothers or male cousins along. During his teens, a boy began hunting with the men, and his father became his teacher.

Haudenosaunee children learned proper behavior by watching adults. They listened carefully to stories told in the longhouses during winter evenings. The stories taught them Haudenosaunee history, customs, and values. There were many stories to encourage good behavior, including one with a creature with a long nose that would carry them off in a big pack basket.

Spirits and Healing

Turtle-shell rattle

Onondaga ceremonial water drum

The Haudenosaunee believe in Orenda, a powerful force that is present in all things. They saw Orenda working each day when the sun rose and when it set. The power was present in the budding spring, the growing corn, the falling leaves, and the snow of winter. At times during the seasons, especially in the winter, unwanted spirits could bring harm to a village. If that happened, a medicine man would perform a ceremony to drive away the unwanted spirits.

At the end of the eighteenth century, after the American Revolutionary War, the Haudenosaunee had lost land to the Americans, sometimes due to fraudulent or coerced treaties. They were struggling because of the white settlers moving into their territories. Traditional customs were giving way to the white men's manner of living. A Seneca medicine man, Ganiodayo, or Handsome Lake, had a vision. He was urged to tell the Haudenosaunee to give up the new beliefs the white men had brought and not drink alcohol. The directions in the vision became the Code of Handsome Lake and were called Gaiwoo, or Good Word. The code described the proper way to marry, how to care for children and the aged, and how to live correctly from birth until death. Many Haudenosaunee became followers of Handsome Lake.

Wampum

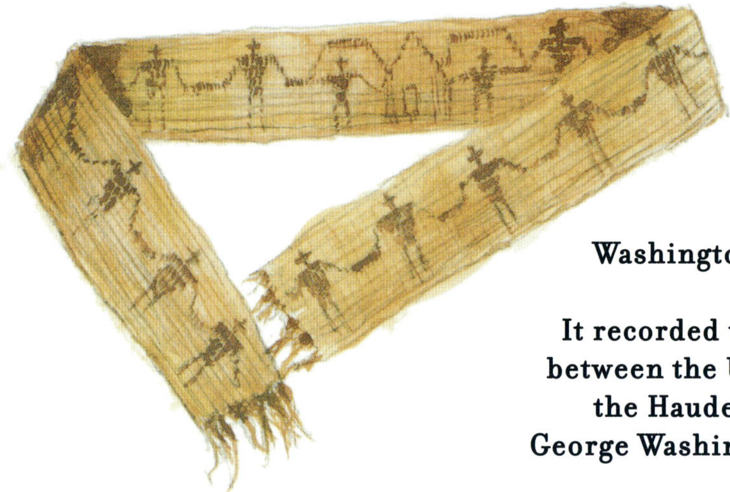

Washington wampum belt

It recorded the treaty of peace between the US government and the Haudenosaunee while George Washington was president.

Wampum belt

Wampum strings

Wampum served many purposes among the Haudenosaunee. The word comes from the Algonquins and means "white strings," because wampum was made from strings of white shell beads. The beads were strung into strands and woven into belts that were several feet long.

The Haudenosaunee traded for wampum or received it as gifts from other Nations. They called the chiefs to council by sending wampum belts. A chief took the belt with him to be admitted into the council. Wampum belts were sent to another Nation with an invitation to join a war. Treaties between Nations and with the white men were recorded on belts made for the occasion.

The wampum belts became public records kept by the Onondaga. Several belts are still in existence and are prized Haudenosaunee treasures, since they are a record of their history.

Europeans used wampum in place of coins, but the Haudenosaunee did not really use wampum as money.

Today

Joseph Brant, a Mohawk war leader who fought against the Americans during the Revolutionary War

General John Sullivan

The Haudenosaunee men were fearless warriors, and the league united them into a powerful force. During the French and Indian War from 1754 to 1763, the Haudenosaunee sided with the British. But, during the American Revolutionary War, from 1775 to 1783, the Haudenosaunee were divided. In 1779, General John Sullivan, under George Washington's orders, destroyed villages who had helped the British, including villages of the Seneca and Cayuga, along with one Onondaga village.

After the war, white men continued to settle on Haudenosaunee land, so the United States government forced many Haudenosaunee people, but not all, to move. US President Andrew Jackson forcibly removed many Native Nations. The Haudenosaunee retained their territories, but their land became smaller. Some Haudenosaunee people did leave to go to Wisconsin, Oklahoma, Kansas, or Canada. Today, the Haudenosaunee do not live on reservations like some other Native Nations. The Haudenosaunee continue to live on their original territory.

Modern longhouse

Today the Oneida have two territories, one in New York State and one in Green Bay, Wisconsin. The Oneida Nation Museum displays a reconstructed village with a longhouse.

Brantford, Ontario, is named for Joseph Brant. It is the site of the Woodland Indian Cultural Education Center, where one can do research on Haudenosaunee culture and history and see modern arts and crafts.

The Six Nations Grand River Indian Reserve in Ontario is home to thousands of Haudenosaunee, mostly Mohawks and Cayugas.

Haudenosaunee children go to schools on their territories as well as in cities and towns where their parents live and work. Some Haudenosaunee are farmers and mechanics. Haudenosaunee steel-construction workers have helped build high bridges, towers, and many skyscrapers in New York City and other cities.

Other Haudenosaunee go to college and become teachers, doctors, lawyers, engineers, and businessmen. There are Haudenosaunee artists, writers, and musicians who keep their heritage alive through their art.

The ancient festivals are still celebrated, and lacrosse is a competitive sport among Indigenous and non-Indigenous people.

Women continue to head traditional clans, and the Haudenosaunee Confederacy continues to meet in a Grand Council.

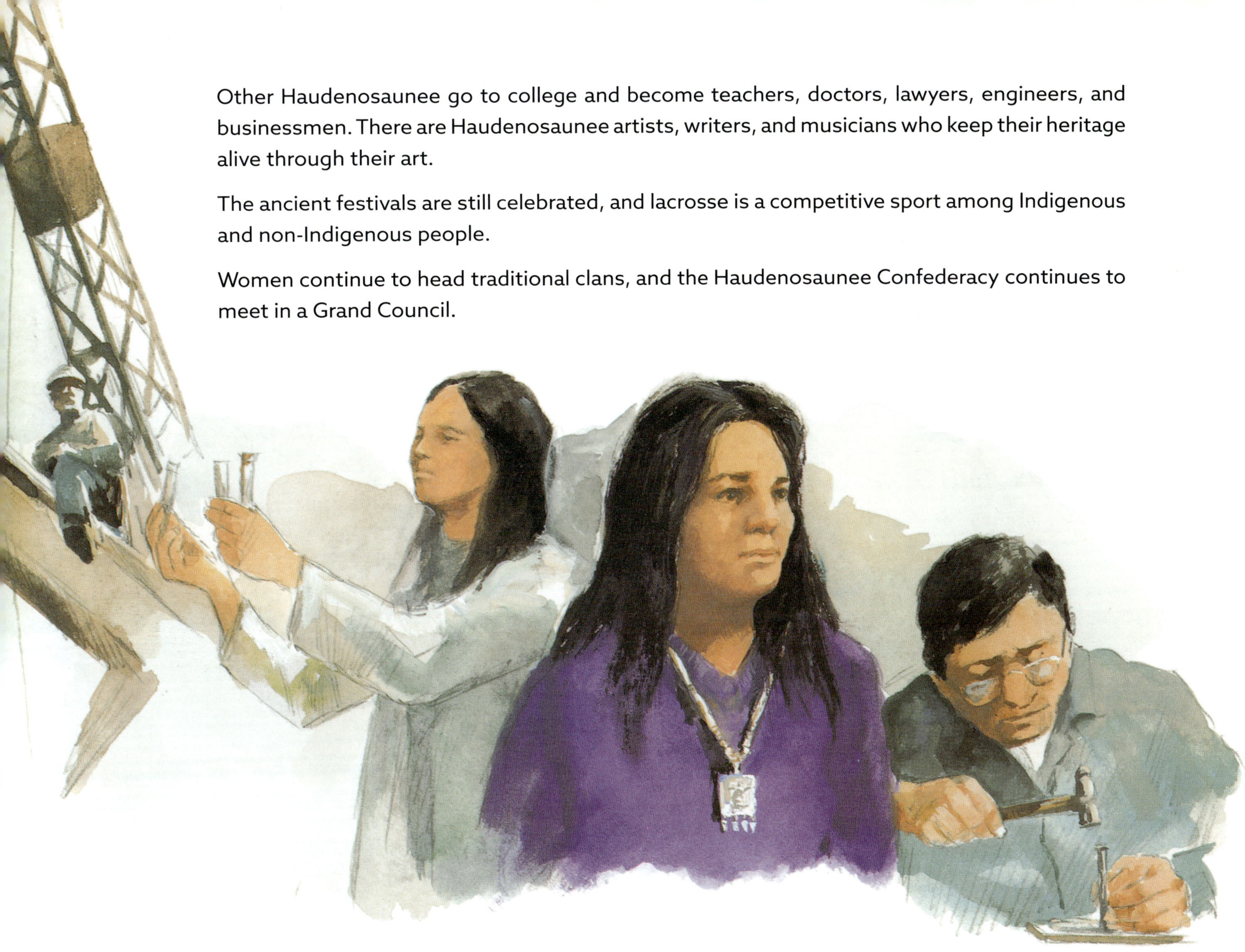

EWY Media / Shutterstock

Wampum belt

Zack Frank / Shutterstock

The Three Sisters Garden, Ganondagan State Historic Site in New York State

Photo courtesy of Hayden Haynes

Cloud Connected (2020) by Hayden Haynes. Hayden Haynes is a Seneca artist who uses traditional carving techniques and imagery in his work. You can learn more at haydensantlercreations.com.

Zack Frank / Shutterstock

Longhouse, Ganondagan State Historic Site in New York State

Zack Frank / Shutterstock

Longhouse interior, Ganondagan State Historic Site in New York State

FOR MORE INFORMATION ON THE HAUDENOSAUNEE

Haudenosaunee Confederacy website: https://www.haudenosauneeconfederacy.com/

Iroquois Museum: https://www.iroquoismuseum.org/

Mohawk Nation website: https://www.srmt-nsn.gov/

New York State Museum, Kanien'keha:ka (Mohawk) Haudenosaunee Village: https://www.nysm.nysed.gov/mohawk-haudenosaunee-village

Oneida Nation websites: https://oneida-nsn.gov/ and https://www.oneidaindiannation.com/

Shako:wi Cultural Center (Oneida): https://www.oneidaindiannation.com/shakowiculturalcenter/

Onondaga Nation website: https://www.onondaganation.org/

Skä•noñh Great Law of Peace Center (Onondaga): https://www.skanonhcenter.org/

Ganondagan State Historic Site (Seneca): https://www.ganondagan.org/

Onöhsagwë:de' Cultural Center (Seneca): https://www.senecamuseum.org/

Seneca-Cayuga Nation (Oklahoma): https://sctribe.com/index.php/

Seneca Nation website: https://sni.org/

MORE RESOURCES ABOUT NATIVE AMERICANS

Indigenous Photograph: https://indigenousphotograph.com

Native American tribe websites: https://libguides.du.edu/c.php?g=90322&p=582788

National Museum of the American Indian: https://americanindian.si.edu

Indian Country Today: https://ictnews.org

AUTHOR'S NOTE

The Hiawatha of the Haudenosaunee is not the Hiawatha of Longfellow's legend.

EXPLORE MORE FIRST NATIONS

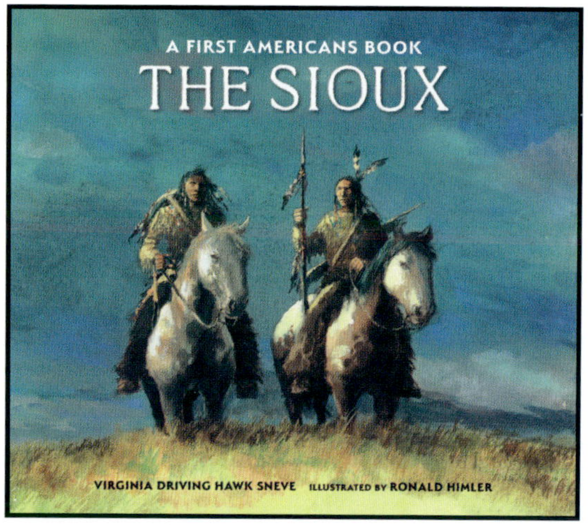

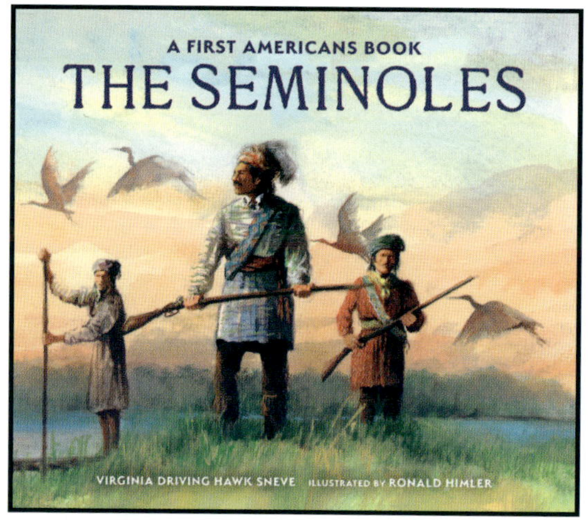

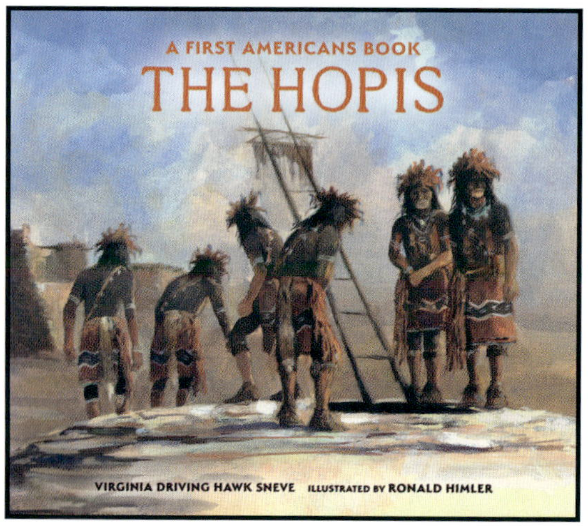

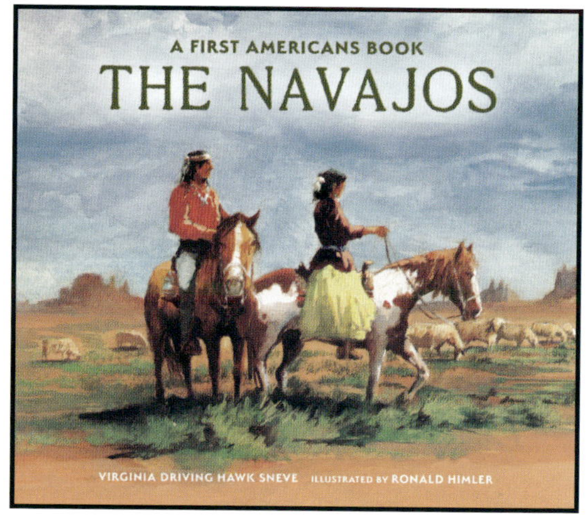